a Moment of Water

Ann Powellmar

a Moment of Water

Journey by Maine Watershed

LANDSCAPE PHOTOGRAPHY & JOURNAL NOTES

Ann Flewelling

a Moment of Water IS AN ARTISTICALLY CURATED SHOW OF PHOTOGRAPHIC MOMENTS ON MAINE WATERWAYS THAT CREATES IN THE VIEWER A DEEPENED SENSE OF CONNECTION TO THE NATURAL LANDSCAPE AND ITS HUMAN WATERSHED.

FLOATSTONE RIVER

I find true friendship in the river.
Every morning I awake
remembering,
eager,

I go down to see her,
sit by her side
and listen, close
for understanding.

Then she gathers the light
and the water between us
and hands me a poem.

To be on the water, to look deep into the moment *and capture an image, is, as I see it, intimate landscape. This private perspective on the natural environment lies quietly within our embrace and offers personal connection to worlds that are both within and beyond us all.*

ACKNOWLEDGMENTS

My husband Charles Read has given enthusiastic support for this book—navigating, hiking, paddling, boating, and driving with me to the Crown of Maine and back Downeast while I photographed. I am grateful for his patience and enduring companionship.

My friend and Threehalf Press partner Marnie Reed Crowell first inspired the creative collaboration that became our independent small press and publisher of this book. I owe the evolution of much of my present skill in creating books to the experience of working with her since 2005 to publish eight artistic books, our combined voice and vision speaking on behalf of the natural environment.

I am fortunate to have inherited my parents' love of Maine's natural landscape; it is a gift continued from past generations.

Special thanks to David S. Cook for his book *Above the Gravel Bar: Indian Canoe Routes of Maine*, 2nd edition, 1985, and for permission to use detail from his charming handmade map of Indian canoe routes. It was my reading of the second edition of his book—inherited from my parent's library (having been given *them* by one of *their* children)—that lead to the native American dimension of my discoveries along my journey on Maine watersheds. Armed with Cook's map and DeLorme's *Maine Atlas*, I found meaningful connections that otherwise might have remained invisible to me.

Without the promotion of watershed protection by local conservation organizations such as Blue Hill Heritage Trust, Bagaduce Watershed Association, Island Heritage Trust, Maine Coast Heritage Trust, and statewide support by the Natural Resources Council of Maine, many of the landscapes reflected in this book might have looked neither lovely nor healthy. The BWA establishment of river and stream team monitoring and its promotion of eelgrass restoration under the early leadership of Nonny Ferriday is progress celebrated along with the protection by IHT of the Lily Pond and Scott's Landing, by BHHT of the Bagaduce Preserve, Peters Brook, and Fourth Pond, and by NRCM for its positive environmental impact statewide. A portion of the proceeds from the sale of this book is donated to non-profit organizations, such as those above, whose efforts help protect Maine's watersheds.

af ~ December 2011

Contents

DEDICATED TO MY PARENTS

Leo Flewelling and Lila Carvell Flewelling

Northern Maine lovers of outdoor life, lore, and landscape—
they passed this on to us, the next generation, in a spirit of trust
that we will do, in our own good ways, the same.

Downstream Perspective

WHEN YOU LOVE A RIVER, LAKE, BROOK, POND, OR BAY, something deep is going on. There seems to be a reflecting dynamic between water and other forces on the landscape—human desire, affinity for connection across families and generations, geography and history, across the whole living landscape, particle-to-particle and cell-to-cell resonating. Full circle.

Water changes the nature of light on the landscape. *A Moment of Water* flows from the powerful sense of connection I feel to this place and the river, deep as time, wide as water, enigmatic as the light floating stones. As I kayak on these waters, it is the balance point of light that holds me captive in its moment, reflecting stone, sky, tree. Water has been beside me wherever I've lived in Maine, place of my childhood home by a river and our family camp on a lake. Now, Downeast, at home in adulthood on a peninsula on a scenic tidal estuary, we see water in all directions: cove on the east, rapids on the west, broad run north downriver nearly 12 miles to Penobscot Bay, a trout pond to the south and, beyond, more cove and river.

No, we don't live on an island, at least not yet, not unless melting polar ice cap makes it so. Even now a heavy spring rain can reduce the low neck of our landed connection to near causeway status, the soaked watershed runoff backlogged, bottlenecked at the reversing falls between here and the bay.

Meanwhile, I listen carefully in the big quiet of water for ancestral sounds, murmur of indigenous people paddling *agwiden* (Penobscot tribe name *"floats lightly"* for the birch bark canoe) all the way down from Northern Maine's Aroostook River, a short carry to water links to the Penobscot, then paddling right past this little peninsula on the Bagaduce en route to Walker Pond, then a carry to the Punch Bowl of Eggemoggin Reach, and off to Deer Isle, or up the Benjamin River to Salt Pond, further on to Blue Hill Bay… Or maybe, just as we are, pausing right here to make camp for a season.

GRAND L

SEBEC R

KASANT R

SEBEC L

PISCATAQUIS R

ONOSBRY STR

SEBASTICOOK R

WESSERUNSETT R

KENDUSKEAG

KENNEBEC R

SEBST. COOK R

SHELDSLER R

PENOBSCOT BAY

PENOBSCOT R

MATTANISIT

PASSADUMKEAG R

OLAMON STR

NICATOUS L

SUNKHAZE STR

MACHIAS R

OLD UNION R

UD. BR.

CRAVAN L

CHEMO STR

NARRAGUAGUS R

*IDENTIFIES

PHOTOGRAPHIC

POINT OF VIEW

~ *from the Downeast Coast* ~

PENOBSCOT BAY AREA

Bagaduce *River*

THE SETTING IS THE SCENIC BAGADUCE, short for Majabigwaduce, *the big tideway river*, flowing into Penobscot Bay. From our home on a small 12 acre peninsula in the Upper Bagaduce, I explore, always camera in hand, by foot and by kayak, the balance point of light on Snow Cove to the east, the 5th Narrows to the west, the view from "North Point," as we name and capitalize it, and south to "The Neck," low connector that joins us to the landed rest.

On this upriver portion of the Bagaduce estuary, the tides and current are modest. On the east shore of the peninsula, Snow Cove, evergreen and deciduous woodland protect the shallow calm cove ("Quiet Cove" we call it) with its eelgrass meadows—marine nurseries—timeless homestead of horseshoe crabs and convenient dining for the great blue heron. On the west shore is the 5th Narrows, a constricted, rock strewn passage with a broad blueberry barren on opposite bank. The flat water of Judy Rapids, as the 5th Narrows is locally known, barely betrays the mild turbulence beneath its surface at flood and ebb tides. Pygmy alewives slip though here on their way to Walker Pond spawning grounds while, overhead, bald eagles glide to alight in favorite spruce perches on North Point.

Our little peninsula's North Point provides a far view down river as it twists out of sight on its course through four more narrows before rejoining the bay.

NORTH POINT ~ *Between Snow Cove and the 5th Narrows*
River of pollen. Inset: eelgrass flower.

The river in winter is more or less frozen in place except for a channel of open water gracefully curving through the Narrows. All of Snow Cove and the far view downriver is a whitescape punctuated by small seasonal cubes of ice fishing shacks. On weekends bundled figures scurry up and down the frozen river like human commas or small smelt.

Some winter nights the river groans, long deep, reverberating tidal moans. "The great river whales…" one of us predicatably wails with knowing glance, the other groaning. South, down at the narrow neck of land, a near sea level stem connects us to the rest of the landed planet. Here, river otters, those shy pups who year-round grace us with playful surprise, body slide from shore to shore—disappear into the culvert and out again on the other side—leaving their trail perpendicular to our snow-plowed drive. Tracking the signs, I muse over the metaphor.

Come spring, on signal with first bloom of shadblow, the osprey return overhead, bright chevrons heralding.

SNOW COVE
April Shadblow

SNOW COVE
Sunrise and river mist

5TH NARROWS
Immature bald eagle, not far from the nest in tallest pine (behind bird),
enjoys its feast of horseshoe crab on the rocks.

5TH NARROWS
Gazing north downriver past these "floatstone islands" usually occupied by ducks, gulls, and herons.
I and my kayak intruding, all have briefly evacuated.
Inset: horseshoe crab mating (Snow Cove).

VIEW FROM "THE NECK" ~ *Upriver from the 5th Narrows*
Spring though fall my walk-by almost every evening produces
a startle of ducks taking flight with *Wings...wings...wings...*, receding muffled thunder-flap of
Womp...womp...womp..., then brilliant grand finale circling overhead... a *whisper...* of wings.

SNOW COVE

Spirit oak waits gracefully to give up its leaves, season of ice again nearing.

5TH NARROWS

Snow, ice, channel flow

5ᵀᴴ NARROWS

Otter tracks in ice slush.

SNOW COVE

Two travellers and a dog on winter river.

Tiny cubes of ice-fishing shacks appear on distant

horizon   .

SNOW COVE

The zigzag give and take of ice-out on this windy April day creates an operatic clatter and clamor—glass music. From my perch high over the river in an oak branch, I have a birds-eye view of what, another river, another time, might have been the great negotiation of log jams in one of Maine's historic river log drives.

SNOW COVE ~ *Blue Hill Heritage Trust Bagaduce River frontage*
From our east shore we gaze at this pristine sight a mere 1000 feet away on opposite shore
of what we call "Quiet Cove." Once slated for residential development, now this beautiful
shoreline—almost 2200 feet of it—is protected thanks to a generous donation in 2007 of a 58
acre tract of land. Drinking in the stunning view, we are grateful, as also is, I like to imagine,
this granite behemoth drinking the pure river light.

SNOW COVE ~ *Bagaduce River frontage, Blue Hill Heritage Trust*
Morning light glides over the big silence of grass ~ water ~ stone.

Soft *chuff chuff* coughing sound behind me.
   I turn.
Ah! A visit from my river buddies.

STONY BROOK INLET ~ *Sedgwick*

Locals fish this stream (DeLorme's *Maine Atlas* calls it *Snow Brook*). Draining the
watershed of a massive blueberry barren, Stony Brook is one of several streams we
monitored for the Bagaduce Watershed Association. Sadly, once when monitoring the
stream, we found a slack carcass of road-kill river otter by the bridge guardrail.

Bluff Head ~ *Sedgwick*

Still paddling north, downriver, past the great ledge known as Bluff Head.
Moments before, we discovered a canoe-size shallow cave in
a north side of ledge. My husband in kayak snugged into the
cave to try it on for size, posed for a picture, then paddled off
to become small speck on the horizon (right page, far left).

3RD NARROWS, BAGADUCE REVERSING FALLS ~ *Brooksville/Sedgwick*

THREAT TO HABITAT LOSS UPRIVER because of migrating stone piers at the bridge here certainly got my attention when I learned about it, three days before this book went to press. I got Bagaduce Watershed Association leaders on the phone. I found that the new 2005 Davis Narrows Bridge replaced one built in 1941 that had received a DOT rating well below the target for bridge replacement—there had been some movement of its stacked granite piles. The new bridge was constructed on precast abutments placed on top of the granite block piles. DOT agreed to leave the existing outlet unchanged to preserve sensitive upriver environments. A missed point, apparently, was the possibility that unused bridge piers might continue to migrate, which they *are* doing, increasing the outlet. Last March a DOT evaluation team pier rating was 3; today, December 6, 2011, their rating is 5. I, too, began moving. The concern is that the increasing flow might result in loss of eelgrass meadows and horseshoe crab as well as pygmy alewife habitat upriver. No more alewives in Walker Pond? No more horseshoe crabs in Snow Cove? Clay mudflats? No, no, no…

2ND NARROWS ~ *Young's Point*

Protected by the Conservation Trust of Brooksville, Penobscot, and Castine, the Snow Natural Area is one where seal sightings are common. The foreground shoreline leads west to a major seal pupping ledge in Green Cove. The large granite boulder (right, forground)points toward tip of barred Green Island (also shown above).

Shore opposite is Johnson Point, Penobscot.

Big Tideway River ~ *Brooksville view across to Castine*

This, photographed at low tide, casts my vote for "Big Tideway River" as the most likely translation of the Penobscot Indian name for the Bagaduce (short for *majabigwaduce*). Just imagine this at high tide! Early *agwiden* (remember *floats lightly,* birch bark canoe) travellers, paddling down the Penobscot's eastern shore, opted for a shortcut carry from Wadsworth Cove to Hatch Cove (marshy colored area far right on opposite shore). Better than taking the long way all around Castine. Arriving at the end of their carry, they would see this waterway—"Big Tideway River" would certainly identify it. Two other translations offered are "at a bad shoal" (upriver at the 2nd Narrows, on previous page, can be difficult to navigate at low tide) and "water bad to drink" *matchibignadusek* (yes, the brackish water is bad to drink). I suspect, however, that native American Indians, experts in outdoor survival and water travel hardly needed special instructions such as "avoid at low tide" or "don't drink the water."

On the horizon left of center are the Hills of Camden and, in Castine Harbor, the *The State of Maine* training ship in its home port. Each summer young crewmates, freshly educated, cruise to oceans far beyond any waters the native Americans had either craft or time enough to explore.

Walker *Pond*

THIS SOFT SAND BEACH MUST DELIGHT THE BARE FEET of young campers from the Blue Hill Peninsula area who swim here at Nichols Day Camps, a non-profit organization whose mission is "To instill in our peninsula area youth a lifelong passion for outdoor recreational and educational experiences." The organization's purpose is "To provide opportunities for area youth to experience our local woods, wind and water through a variety of life skills. These opportunities will use the natural resources of Maine's beauty to promote confidence and self-esteem." The founder, Francis T. Nichols, "believed that all area children should learn to swim and learn to appreciate the out-of-doors, especially in a simple, rustic camp setting. He also believed no child should be denied these opportunities for financial reasons. During his lifetime his generosity sustained this vision. In 1979 he and others established a permanent camp site on Walker Pond."

WALKER POND ~ *Outlet near old Indian village, Brooksville*
The village was burned, a site of mutual depredations—native American Indian on white man,
white man on native American. Legend has it, and archeological remains—including charcoal black
soil, arrowheads, spearheads, and human remains—support an old Indian village existing near here
on Walker Pond on the beautiful south-sloping shore slightly west of the present day beaver dam
and downstream fish ladder. This was an Indian canoe carry area to and from the Bagaduce River.
As Bagaduce Stream Team monitors testing down-ladder from here, we were often thrilled
by large late afternoon assaults from hungry great blue herons.

Lily *Pond*

LILY POND HAS BEEN A FAMILY FAVORITE FOR SWIMMING and fishing for generations of the residents of Deer Isle as well as for visitors who learn how to find this precious spot. In 2010 The Island Heritage Trust, after many years of private negotiations, acquired this beach section of the pond and maintains its use.

Fourth *Pond*

ONE OF ONLY A FEW UNDEVELOPED PONDS on the coast of Maine, this 50 acre pond in Blue Hill
is protected by Blue Hill Heritage Trust. A peek at DeLorme's *Maine Atlas* will show the pond's
connection to Third, Second, and First ponds, then via both Duck Marsh and Carlton Streams to Salt
Pond, which is connected by water north to Blue Hill Bay as well as south to the Benjamin River then
to Eggemoggin Reach. Seems like possibly an Indian coastal canoe side trip—perhaps for fresh water
fishing, hunting, and fur trapping?

FaRview Farm *Pond*

EVENINGS WE WATCH THE QUIET SURFACE of our farm pond, empathy neurons firing with contentment as we imagine the satisfaction of rainbow trout feeding.

Peters *Brook*

A HIKE ALONG THE PETERS BROOK TRAIL REFRESHES THE SOUL. Another Blue Hill Heritage Trust site, this brook, shedding water from the upland area east of Blue Hill village, flows into Peters Cove and Blue Hill Bay. A moderately steep half-mile trail hike upstream terminates with reward of a waterfall.

Water from Peters Brook ziggurats into Peters Cove to Blue Hill Bay

A keen eye, following watery zig-zag dotted with shore birds, will find a great blue heron at the head (find the dot between far dark rock and boat on right.) Blue Hill Heritage Trust has a small shorefront lot providing public parking and historic access to Blue Hill Bay.

Peters Brook
Pool. Inset: long view upstream.

Blue Hill *Bay* & Eggemoggin *Reach*

CLASSIC BLUE HILL VILLAGE AND HARBOR hold such charm. Though the Blue Hill area may technically, I suppose, not officially be a part of Penobscot Bay, I like to include it—just as I imagine *agwiden* travellers did as well—all of these waters *so* connected.

EGGEMOGGIN REACH ~ *Deer Isle (Scott's Landing)*
The suspension of the present day Sedgwick–Deer Isle bridge points on the west (left) horizon.

EGGEMOGGIN REACH ~ Sedgwick *(Billings Cove)*
South-pointing ledge directs the eye to the north shore of Deer Isle at both Scott's Landing, an Island Heritage Trust preserve, and Old Ferry Landing. Surely early canoe travellers, gazing across time, share the view with us. Watch carefully... you may see *agwiden*...

Penobscot *River*

Downriver from the Penobscot Narrows Bridge ~ *Bucksport*

You might see Gluskabe mightily paddling his stone canoe upriver against the current—bet he wishes he had an *agwiden*. Curious? Turn page for revelation.

Historic Fort Knox and Contemporary Bucksport on the Penobscot

Penobscot Narrows Bridge Observatory view of river festivites on opening day 2007.

Gluskabe's River

by Marnie Reed Crowell
Commissioned for the opening of Penobscot Narrows Bridge ~ 2007

All the night long
as the storm tracks by,
southerly winds from out at sea
push ocean back into the bay.
Hear Gluskabe
paddling by in his stone canoe,
the shouts and smacks
as he urges the Penobscot back,
back by waves,
past the Eggemoggin Reach,
on beyond the quiet Bagaduce,
under the place where the sinewed seam
stitches bank to bank,
beyond Bangor,
rippling round Indian Island,
on to Orono, to Millinocket,
threading through Maine Woods,
till pure and clear
what's left of water
—clouds—
reach Wabanaki heart,
Katahdin,
and regroup
for yet another schussing run
downriver through the towns and mills,
out to dawn
and sea.

PENOBSCOT RIVER ~ *View from Fort Point State Park, Stockton Springs*
Small sparkling span on the far left horizon is the great Penobscot Narrows bridge

SANDY POINT ~ *Stockton Springs*

Penobscot River continues its journey past the rotting pilings of what was once a ferry pier (right horizon), remnants now part of Sandy Point State Park. Entering the river (right) between distant pilings and shore marsh is Muskrat Stream, outflow from Muskrat Pond, formerly site of a commercial muskrat fur business, now part of the Stowers Meadow—Maine Wildlife Management Area.

Bordered by the Penoboscot River and Marsh Stream, Treat Point, a 91 acre wooded preserve, is protected by the Maine Department of Inland Fisheries and Wildlife. Its acquisition was negotiated though Maine Coast Heritage Trust. A diverse productive ecosystem and large intertidal marsh, it is a Penobscot River tributary (entrance shown right of center).

Killdeer, below, in parking lot mud puddle, introduced himself to me.
"Ann, here" I replied.

Mount
Katahdin

Inset: View of the heart of
the Northern Appalachians

Salmon Stream lake

* IDENTIFIES

PHOTOGRAPHIC

POINT OF VIEW

via the Katahdin ~ Watershed Region

Salmon Stream *Lake*

THERE IS SOMETHING ABOUT MOUNT KATAHDIN—a desire for primal connection to the wildscape—that draws us to this place along with all the other travellers who pull off I-95 to check out the overlook. People are always taking pictures and posing in the view to have their picture taken, proving *I have been here, in this place with its glistening lake filled by watershed of the great spirit mountain.*

Years ago my father painted a headressed chieften profile on the left side of the bow of his 20 foot Old Town Guide canoe and an indian princess with feathered headband on the right, symbols for he and my mother travelling together. This Thanksgiving I showed my elderly father an online video, *Agwiden—Building a Birch Bark Canoe,* which I'd discovered in the process of building this book. In 2005 Chief Barry Dana hired Steve Cayard, a white man, to show tribal members how to regain their lost art of *agwiden* building—one hour of moving moments from birch bark harvest all the way to launch captured in a digital video ending with Elder placing feathers onto the bow, tribal members lifting the light *agwiden* into the Penobscot. In one graceful motion barefoot Chief steps in and kneels, dipping ash paddle in the sacred river, and glides into the big quiet of water. Beside me came soft murmer of my father's voice full of reverence and delight, "Oh, that is so… Beautiful!" I folded my hands to silent lips, smiling and weeping.

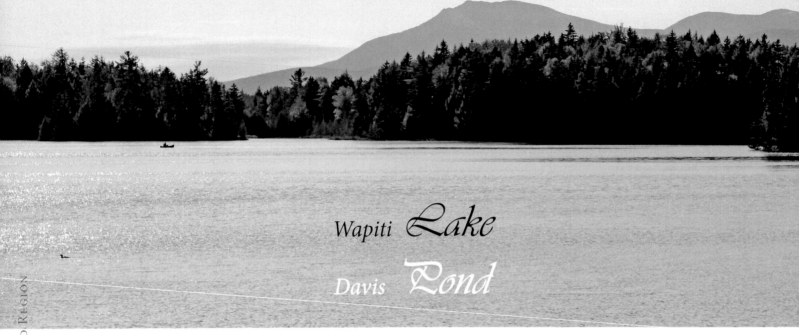

Wapiti *Lake*

Davis *Pond*

THIS QUIET SUNDAY DURING BLACK BEAR SEASON served up this timeless scene—canoe, loon, mountain. *Wapiti* is the name given the lake by two school teachers from Bangor who built the Camp Wapiti lodge and cabins in 1917 on the shore on which I am standing. *Wapiti* is the early American word for *elk, caribou*—this according to one of the two current Maine Guide owners of this now sporting resort, who prefers the DeLorme's *Maine Atlas* map designation, Davis Pond.

Whether lake or pond, native trout swim in its waters that flow into the Seboeis River, which links me to my childhood home along the Aroostook River in "The County," the Crown of Maine.

Shin *Pond*

Upper and Lower Shin Ponds flow into the Seboeis River. The seaplane on Lower Shin Pond (far right on opposite page) offers scenic airplane rides and fly-in fishing and canoe trips on the region's remote lakes.

SHIN POND FALLS

From below and above. Here is where friends come in. I was photographing the Seboeis River from a remote bridge when the only car drove by, slowed, and pulled onto the shoulder next to ours. What are the chances? Maine license plate FARVIEW next to FLOWRS, friends from the Blue Hill peninsula. They exploring "the fold in the map" first time ever, we first time visitors here, too. We in search of Shin Falls, they having just hiked there. They looking for Sawtell Falls, we having just passed it. Favors exchanged, all travelled on and, gratis connection, and we found Shin Falls. ALL THINGS APART FALL TOGETHER.

Seboeis *River*

THE SEBOEIS *small brook* River link became important in my exploration of connections—geographic, historic, and otherwise. How did I get here from there on this journey to discover all that connects me to my origins along the Aroostook River to the place I now love on the Bagaduce River. We visited here after discovering in Cook's book that native people from what is now Northern Maine and Canada poled an upriver route of the Aroostook to a tributary, Lapomkeag (*crooked stream*), then to West Carry Branch, then a half mile carry to Grand Lake Seboeis to paddle down the Seboeis River to the East Branch of the Penobscot. This waterway connection gave access to summer hunting and gathering on the downeast coast via the Penobscot to the Bagaduce, to Walker Pond, to the Punch Bowl on Eggemoggin Reach, to the Benjamin River to Salt Pond to Blue Hill Bay, Peters Brook flowing into it. And, of course, so much more water to explore…

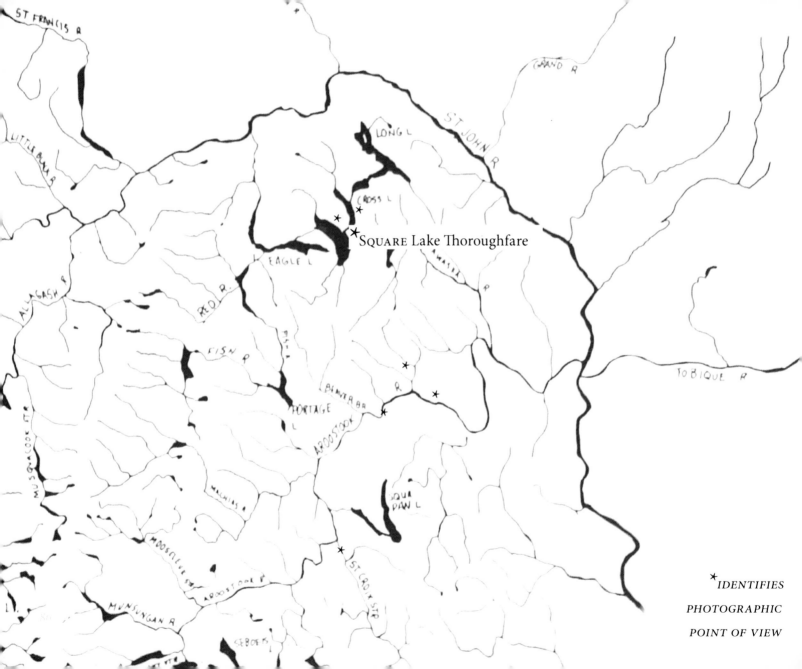

SQUARE Lake Thoroughfare

*IDENTIFIES

PHOTOGRAPHIC

POINT OF VIEW

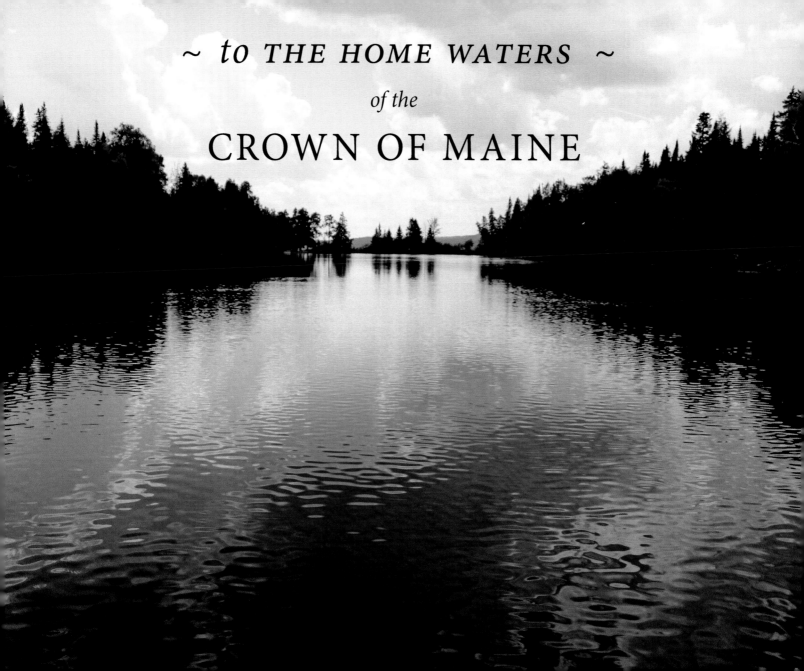

~ *to* THE HOME WATERS ~

of the

CROWN OF MAINE

Aroostook *River*

I GREW UP IN A FARMING COMMUNITY along the Aroostook *(beautiful)* River. The river valley provided the rich soil of our livelihood. We played beside the river, cut ash saplings for fishing poles rigged with string and safetypin hooks—worms free for the digging from the river bank—caught chub and planted our fishy catch under the garden corn. We swam in the river's *Little Deep Hole* and were baptized in the *Big Deep Hole*. My father, uncles, grandfathers, great uncles, and great grandfathers all farmed this land.

From the time I was five, I, like all of the children released from school each fall for "potato picking," joined in the harvest until crops were stored, as also was our potato picking money—earned barrel by barrel, 25 cents at a time—tenth of the total tithed, a tiny bit set aside for family Christmas, and the bulk saved in the bank for college.

Winter ice melt would overflow the riverbanks and flood the flat fertile fields most every spring, another year beginning and more family crew coming aboard.

The Bidou, below, as I (fifteen) photographed it from behind our great Uncle Willie and Aunt Peryl Crouse's barn and house just across the road from our childhood home in Crouseville. Above, *The Bidou* today. Between flat field and distant ridge lies the lovely Aroostook River.

Meditations on a Fertile Field

Fall plowed under new spring soil, I stand on this flat earth beside the Aroostook, same river that once gathered our fore-fathers-mothers, brought them down the St John from Canada and settled them in the rich loam of this promised land. "The Flat" these fertile fields have always been called.

Here on the surface of our history, I have returned to take trilliums and shards from this familiar ground. Stooping, kneeling, and picking the harvest from Aroostook soil is ours by both birthright and labor of family farm. This is the second advent of the gathering of the trillium this year, my brother having just dug here before me. There is plenty.

I kneel on the river bank—downhill from the village, church at its heart—to resurrect three trilliums, shy memories flowering from this tangled site lost in the overgrowth of forgotten conversations, generations fading away in lost shadows of potato houses, school, steeple, store, barns. Church sanctuary remains awash in window stain: son kneeling alone in the garden of the valley of the shadow, praying to the father before giving up the ghost. I wholly bag the trinity, tuck it tenderly away. I walk on the brown ground of the homestead vanished, stoop to gather a gratitude of shards, rub damp soil from each fragment, looking for some brief memory long forgotten before my birth. I observe: tea cup, chamber pot, vase, bottle, jar. Window pane, horse tooth, small bronze bell. Hand opens: I observe gravity as all returns to the soft remembrance of earth.

I wander the swollen river bank in search of the "Big Deep Hole," watery grave of our sins, site of soul salvation. It is gone from this green valley, channels changing while the baptizing river forever flows, washing along with all my sins, memories away.

St Croix Stream ~ *Masardis*
One of the many tributaries, December and year-round, creating the
downstream broad flow of the Aroostook in Crouseville and beyond.

Aroostook River ~ *Wade*
Autumn in Aroostook, potato harvest done, becomes yet another reason
why this river is beautiful.

Salmon *Brook*

THREE MILES FROM MY CHILDHOOD home in Crouseville, once called East Washburn, I took formal swimming lessons here in the Washburn swimming pool, site of original settler Issac Wilder's mill, dammed stream its source, in the town then known as Salmon Brook. I already knew how to swim, but a formal education is always good, goose poop not withstanding.

Later in life my parents championed the cause of fundraising to save the Wilder homestead as a Salmon Brook Historical Society museum, its deep collections rich today with entrusted local family heritage. The historical society struggles now however—like the few surviving salmon here—the museum mostly closed and original members tired and aging, spawned young far away and far too busy.

Cross Lake

YOUR MOTHER AND I WERE CURIOUS about Cross Lake so we put the 20 foot Old Town Guide canoe up onto the pickup and went exploring. The woods road followed the thoroughfare then branched down to Priest Point—the camp there was once a Catholic priest retreat. So we parked next to there and made our way through the tangle of hazel bushes to the shore, a nice gentle sloping beach, and put in. The lake was quiet and nobody was around—at that time there were very few camps on the lake. I'll never forget our surprise when suddenly an old fellow with boots way up to his knees showed up walking along Priest Point. "Hello," I called out. "Where you headed?" Old fellow said he was walking back to Square Lake. Following the old woods phone line, single line run on spruce trees, all the way from Guerrette down the Mud Lake thoroughfare, around Cross Lake east and south shores, then up the Square Lake thoroughfare to Fraser's Sporting Camps. Turned out the fellow with boots on was old Gordon Fraser himself, walking all the way back to his Sporting Camps on Square. Ordinarily in those days the only way to get to Square, other than by boat or the long way around on foot, was to fly in. "Well," I said, "hop in, we'll take you over; save you some time." I had the motor on the canoe. I'll never forget those beautiful boots way up to his knees—he was an old lumberman, knew he would be walking through some pretty swampy country the way he was going. So we took him over. The dining room at Fraser's Camps always had fresh cedar boughs lining the walls, it smelled so good. They even had lobster on the menu—flew it in.

When we returned to the Cross Lake beach to take out, your mother said, "We should find out if this lot is for sale." So we stopped at old Norman St Peter's store in Guerrette and asked. "It's two lots and their not for sale," Norm said, "but you can lease them. Ninety-nine year lease, renewable. Here's the number to call." So we did. And then in the spring, right after your twin brothers were born—we'd had a good potato harvest the previous fall as well—I brought my hired man up to the lake with me and we built the camp.

Inset: BIG LAKE, *1935*
My father in the stern; in the bow, my mother.

THE LAST TIME MY FATHER TOOK ME FISHING was a quiet morning across the lake from our camp. "They should be biting here," he murmured, idling the motor. He passed a fishing rod to me then cast his own and began trolling, soft motor the only sound accompanying the silence of our shared reverie.

Two loons swam into view. Dad tapped my shoulder, pointing. I nodded.
The water here is dark, deep.

Finally, curiosity could not keep silent. "…Dad, how many quarts of water are there in Cross Lake?"
"Oh, quite a lot," my father answered softly.

"Um, how many quarts are there in a cubic foot?"
"Well, I'd say a cubic foot might fill a milk pail."

"Maybe 12 quarts?"
"Close enough."

"Cross Lake is about 6 miles long and 1 mile wide, right?"
"Uh huh."

"About how deep is the lake?"
"On average I'd say 40 feet, give or take a few."

"… Dad, could you hold this number in your head for me. It's backwards, so switch it:… zero… eight… six… two… three."

"… Three… two… six… eight… zero."

"… times 12… OK, now could you hold this number but switch it: … zero… six… one…two… nine… three."

"… Three… nine… two… one… six… zero."

"… times 40… zero… zero… two… seven… eight… six… five… one… Fifteen million, six hundred eight-seven thousand, two hundred quarts of water in Cross Lake! What do you think of that?

"Well, there certainly is enough."

A wonderful silence…

"Dad… how high have you ever seen the lake?"
"Oh, ice out, water inside the woods' edge sometimes."

"Well… what's the lowest you've ever seen it?"
… My father idled the motor and reeled in our lines. "Not so low that fish would notice."

We motored on back to camp, a single nibble between us.

BOULDERS WERE DEPOSITED LONG AGO in this Square Lake thoroughfare, which flows from Cross Lake into Square. In low water seasons, most boaters through here travel on *slow*, sighting for the boulders lest boat gets a scraped or dented hull, or worse, a bent or broken propeller.

Since a kid I've always gladly volunteered for *rock watch* assignment, leaning forward from, or sitting on, the bow of our boat, sighting and pointing out huge stone shadows as we'd navigate this beautiful half mile waterway to the wild, big water of largely unpopulated Square Lake.

I think now my motivation was not so much out of concern for scratch or ding to the boat that floated us, rather an excuse to focus deep and say what I saw. Or perhaps both are the same thing. I still persist in volunteering for the position even in high water season, the view from the bow so enchanting.

*Post Script: This placid view, captured August 19th, 2011, is not always so. Witness four days later a video published on YouTube showing this same view from the red bow of a boat **speeding** past here toward the former Fraser Camps then the entrance of Square Lake (see image in this book on page 87 introducing this HOME WATERS ~ CROWN OF MAINE section.) The driver? None other than bold eighty-nine year old Norman St Peter himself! Probably having navigated through this thoroughfare from the time he was a kid, now with about eight decades of experience under his belt, Norm really does **know**—better!*

Square *Lake*

BOATING OVER TO SQUARE MEANT THE ADVENTURE of finding limestone fossils, red-green-gray jasper, and best of all, visiting the Hermit Swede's camp. From the solitude of his campsite on Square Lake he shared a vantage point of the graceful hills between us and Soldier Pond, Eagle Lake, St Froid, Fish River, and Portage Lake, same hills that our eyes rested on from our own camp on Cross Lake. As a youth and young adult, if it appeared the Hermit Swede was not there, with my father I would cautiously violate the Hermit Swede's sanctuary to explore his story. Highest on his wooded slope, a cedar pole lean-to. Next, an open air table with the grand privacy of a spruce-framed wild lake view. I loved his perspective on the world and his wisdom in choosing to camp on this shore. Down at woods' edge, hidden in spruce-spill forest floor, the moss-covered cedar lid of his inground cool box, underground brook flowing through it. Fresh fish for supper.

This year, exploring to find his place again, we discovered who the Hermit Swede was, Square Lake Pioneer, and why he disappeared—stone and bench hidden in woods' edge.

RE-ENTERING CROSS LAKE

The reflective serenity of this lakescape remains, for the moment, undisturbed.

Not even our family camp (mere dot on far shore) calls for attention.

CROSS LAKE THOROUGHFARE

This thoroughfare is shallow with small dams.

We always canoe or kayak upstream a half mile to the bridge and rocky shoals, then let the current carry us back, paddle in water only as rudder.

CROSS LAKE

A family of ducks paddle homeward along our shore, waxing crescent moon and Venus guiding.

THERE ARE MOMENTS WHEN I GAZE UPON THE WATER, rapt in reverie—awed at the fluid grace with which water fits into the landscape, the force of its presence, music of its motion, mysterious way its surface reflects the truth and beauty that water sees.

Surely water is a Spirit…

Upstream Perspective

We also journey homeward, returning as early evening descends, to make camp on this shore
for the rest of our lives.
We are together in the big quiet, this liquid moment of water,
agwiden and kayak floating lightly.

Not that it fill until spilling.
Not that it glisten.
Only that it be
enough.

Human Watershed ~ a family on a lake

FAMILY CAMP AT CROSS LAKE ~ *an idea born at Big Lake*
Our parents spent their honeymoon at Big Lake, where they loved to fish,
my mother having caught this nice one.

Finished building their family with a grand finale of twin boys,
our parents celebrated by building a family camp at Cross Lake.

Inset, top, page opposite: A few years ago, after he sold his canoe with his chieften and princess profiles
on the bow, my father mounted identical paintings—symbols of him and my mother travelling and
flourishing together—on a piece of wood, an abundant wheat sheaf burned between them like the bow
of a canoe, parting water. His lovingly crafted plaque now hangs in the family camp.

~ a Family Watershed ~

About the Photographer

ANN FLEWELLING HAS BEEN CAPTURED BY VISUAL IMAGES of the natural world since childhood. The rural Maine landscape first became the focus of her Kodak Brownie Hawkeye then her used Agfa 35mm camera. Years, any number of cameras, and a digital revolution later, Ann's photographic eye clarifies its meditative vision, still holding in view the natural world, its changing light, and the growing perspective of years.

She formally studied photography and related arts at The Southeastern School of Photographic Arts, The Maine Photographic Workshops, and Haystack Mountain School of Crafts. Driven by curiosity and an inclination for active experimentation, she has been engaged in informal study since childhood. An introspective myope with a propensity to focus on the big world of little-noticed landscapes, by high school Ann had begun exploring microphotography of snowflakes, a fascination evolving into a science fair project that ultimately took her to the State science fair competition. Though little noticed then—snowflakes no competition among the storm of 60's brainy-boy computer projects—today Ann shows her digital photography online and in local Maine venues, stores, galleries, and farmers markets.

Since 2005 she has engaged in a collaboration exploring voice and vision with writer-poet Marnie Reed Crowell. Together they formed an independent small press, Threehalf Press. This event became the impetus for Ann to expand her visual and technical horizons to include the world of digital book design. Ann's photographic images as well as her aesthetic sensitivity and digital design skills appear in the Threehalf Press publications *Shared Light on Penobscot Bay, Beads & String: a Maine island pilgrimage, Shore Lines, The Coast of May, A Sky of Birds,* and *Island Meditation.*

In 2008 Ann's work was included in the "My Favorite Maine" show juried by Carl Little as well as the Maine Photography Show juried by Joyce Tenneson. A practicing clinical psychologist and native Mainer, Ann lives with her husband on the shore of the Bagaduce River, a scenic tidal estuary.

www.annflewelling.com

Notes and Links

Map details in this book are taken from a map by David S. Cook, ***Above the Gravel Bar, Indian Canoe Routes of Maine,*** 2nd Edition, 1985, printed by the Milo Printing Company, Milo, Maine. A full size map from this original print was included, folded, in a pocket inside the back cover of the 2nd Edition. The map image used in *A Moment of Water* is reproduced from a digital photograph I made of an acetate print provided me for that purpose by David S. Cook. The image was then altered by converting it to a black and white image from which map place numbers referring to pages in Cook's book were digitally removed. Cook's *Above the Gravel Bar,* 3rd Edition has revised text, but does not feature this particular map. The 3rd edition can be found at www.polarbearandco.com/books/david_cook/index.htm.

PAGE 13: ***Agwiden***, Penobscot name ***floats lightly*** for the paper birch canoe. Why is *lightly* added? Isn't just *floats* enough? Ah, no, of course not! Not for inland Maine river travel by watersheds that can be especially swift in spring melt and rainy seasons. To leave home for a season *and* to be able to return again, it is essential that a craft be light enough to travel *both* ways—to pole upstream against the flow as well as to paddle downstream. Without the coastal advantage of daily changing tides, dug outs, heavier craft, were too cumbersome to allow efficient travel by Maine's inland waterways. The a*gwiden* upstream/downstream survival principle applies, I've learned, on other practical and metaphoric levels, as well.

Page 76: The video ***Agwiden - Building a Birch Bark Canoe*** can be found on www.vimeo.com by searching "agwiden" (vimeo.com/21936011). For more on Steve Cayard visit www.stevecayard.com.

Page 102: The video ***Square Lake Thoroughfare (how to nagivate)*** [sic] can be found on www.youtube.com by searching "Square Lake."

Blue Hill Heritage Trust
www.bluehillheritagetrust.org

Island Heritage Trust
www.islandheritagetrust.org

Natural Resources Council of Maine
www.nrcm.org

Maine Coast Heritage Trust
www.mcht.org

The Conservation Trust of Brooksville, Penobscot, and Castine
www.theconservationtrust.net

For information on the Bagaduce Watershed
www.coa.edu/gisbagaducewatershed.htm
www.maine.gov/doc/nrimc/mnap/focusarea/bagaduce_river_focus_area.pdf

Nichols Day Camps
www.nicholsdaycamps.org

Also by THREEHALF PRESS

Shared Light on Penobscot Bay (2007)

Beads & String, a Maine island pilgrimage (2008)

Mark Island Light (2009)

Shore Lines (2010)

The Coast of May (2010)

Great Blue, Odyssey of a Heron (2011)

A Sky of Birds, images from Downeast Audubon (2011)

Island Meditation (2011)

a Moment of Water: Upstream ~ Downstream   a April 2012 – October 2013 Calendar (2011)

www.threehalfpress.net